Go Programming for Network Operations

A Golang Network Automation Handbook

Tom McAllen, CCIE 26867

Table of Contents

About the Author

Tom McAllen is a developer and network expert with over two decades of experience in programming and network operations. He began his career as a Linux Admin and Web Application Developer and after an internship at Merit Network and the North American Network Operators Group (NANOG) he went on to complete a Bachelors in Computer Science and Masters in Technology Management. Tom also holds over a dozen active technical certifications that include Cisco Certified Internetwork Expert (CCIE) and Certified Information Systems Security Professional (CISSP). Today he works in Austin, TX at a Fortune Global 500 enterprise as a Senior Principal Network Engineer.

Disclaimer

The information provided in this book is for educational purposes only. The reader is responsible for his or her own actions. While all attempts have been made to verify the information provided in this book, the author does not assume any responsibility for errors, omissions, or contrary interpretations of the subject matter contained within. The author does not accept any responsibility for any liabilities or damages, real or perceived, resulting from the use of this information.

All trademarks and brands within this book are for clarifying purposes only, are owned by the owners themselves, and are not affiliated with this document. The trademarks used are without any consent, and the publication of the trademark is without permission or backing by the trademark owner.

Introduction

Go is the most exciting new mainstream programming language to appear in recent decades. Like modern network operations, Go has taken aim at 21st century infrastructures, particularly in the cloud. This book illustrates how to apply Go programming to network operations. The topics cover common use cases through examples that are designed to act as a guide and serve as a reference.

The reader is assumed to have already gained a fundamental understanding of Go programming; however, the examples are explained for additional clarification. The focus is on using Go for network operations, not on the language itself. This book's approach is practical; readers are encouraged to experiment with the examples and piece together their own programs to gain hands-on experience.

The examples in this book are designed for print copy format. They are short and concise, while maintaining enough content to run and illustrate the point. While error handling is omitted for brevity, it is always recommended to include it, along with other best practices, when developing production code.

Why Go for Network Operations?

The Go programming language is a modern language released in 2009 by an internal team at Google. As an engineered language (rather than something that evolved over time), Go comes with several key advantages. It uses a clean and easy-to-understand syntax that avoids the complexity of other languages, such as C++. It is statically typed, yet efficient by supporting short variable declaration, interfaces, and structural typing.

Another key advantage is built-in concurrency at the core of the language. The Go concurrency model is simple and effective by leveraging goroutines and channels, rather than less efficient threads. Concurrency is native to the language and scales efficiently as the number of CPU cores increase.

Go is lightweight and fast. It is directly compiled to binary rather than depending on an interpreter. This unlocks the performance of running directly on the underlying hardware, while reducing the overhead through its inherent garbage collection. Compilation is fast; therefore, it is practical to use in situations where interpreted languages are normally used. It conveniently compiles to a single binary file and can cross-compile for several operating systems and architectures, including MacOS, Linux, Windows, and BSD.

The rise in popularity and adoption in Go clearly demonstrates its benefit in the real world of IT. The next-generation features that are engineered into the language from the beginning can increase confidence when relying on it for production use. As networks continue to evolve and companies look more at programmability and automation to address new challenges, network operations must remain agile using a modern set of tools.

1

File and Directory Basics

Files and directories are a fundamental feature of most operating systems. The ability to manipulate and interpret them is an essential skill. This chapter focuses on several examples that demonstrate basic file and directory operations.

First, this section looks at the fundamentals of opening and closing, and adding and removing files. Then, it covers getting attributes of files, such as size, permissions, ownership and modification date. Finally, the last two sections demonstrate listing files and directories, both in the same directory and recursively.

This chapter will cover the following file and directory topics:

- Opening and closing
- Adding and removing
- Getting information
- Listing directory contents
- Walking a file and directory tree

1.1 Open/Close

There are two main options for opening files, the os.Open() function, that simply accepts a filename and provides a ready-only file, and a more enhanced option, the os.OpenFile() function , which enables more control by implementing the flags depicted in the table below. These flags can be combined by separating them with the logical OR pipe operator.

Flag	Description
O_RDONLY	Open the file read-only.
O_WRONLY	Open the file write-only.
O_RDWR	Open the file read-write.
O_APPEND	Append data to the file when writing.
O_CREATE	Create a new file if none exists.
O_EXCL	Used with O_CREATE. The file must not exist.
O_SYNC	Open for Synchronous I/O.
O_TRUNC	If possible, truncate the file when opened.

The example below demonstrates the more enhanced option by using the os.OpenFile() function to return a pointer to a value of type os.File. The flag combination creates a write-only file if none exists, otherwise, it appends to the file. The os.File.Write() method is then called on the os.File object to append a byte slice to the file. Finally, the os.File.Close() method is called on the os.File object to render the I/O unusable.

```
package main

import "os"

func main() {
```

```
    file, _ := os.OpenFile("file.txt",
        os.O_APPEND|os.O_CREATE|os.O_WRONLY, 0644)

    file.Write([]byte("append data\n"))
    file.Close()
}
```

1.2 Add/Remove

This next example demonstrates adding a directory and file, then removing them. The example starts out by declaring a directory path and file name. Then, leveraging the directory path and setting permission bits, the os.MkdirAll() function is used to create the directory named path. Once the directory is created, the full directory path is built by calling the filepath.Join() function together with the path name. This full path is then used as a parameter in the os.Create() function to create the file and return an os.File object. At this point, the os.File.Close() method is called to close the file and then remove it with the os.Remove() function. Finally, the directory is deleted using the os.RemoveAll() function, which removes the path and any dependent children.

```go
package main

import (
    "os"
    "path/filepath"
)

func main() {
    dpath := "./dir"
    fname := "file.txt"

    _ = os.MkdirAll(dpath, 0777)

    fpath := filepath.Join(dpath, fname)

    file, _ := os.Create(fpath)

    file.Close()

    _ = os.Remove(fpath)

    _ = os.RemoveAll(dpath)
}
```

1.3 Get Info

Getting information from files and directories is straightforward using the os package. This example leverages the os.Stat() function to return an os.FileInfo object that is then used to read various attributes that include file name, size, permissions, last modified timestamp, and whether it is a directory or not. The os.FileInfo object is then used on the respective methods to retrieve the file and directory metadata.

```go
package main

import (
    "fmt"
    "os"
)

func main() {
    file, _ := os.Stat("main.go")

    fl := fmt.Println
    fl("File name: ", file.Name())
    fl("Size in bytes: ", file.Size())
    fl("Last modified: ", file.ModTime())
    fl("Is a directory: ", file.IsDir())

    ff := fmt.Printf
    ff("Permission 9-bit: %s\n", file.Mode())
    ff("Permission 3-digit: %o\n", file.Mode())
    ff("Permission 4-digit: %04o\n",file.Mode())
}
```

There are three different permission representations in the output below that take their form in the standard Unix 9-bit format, 3-digit octal, and 4-digit octal format. These permission bits are formatted using the fmt package string and base integer verbs. Also, take note that the os.FileInfo.ModTime() method returns a time.Time object which is ideal for additional parsing and formatting.

```
File name: main.go
Size in bytes: 0
Last modified: 2018-10-20 10:51:12.305 -0500 EDT
Is a directory: false
Permission bits: -rwxr--r--
Permission 3-digit octal: 744
Permission 4-digit octal: 0744
```

1.4 List Directory Content

Listing directory contents within a specific directory can be implemented using one of the I/O utility functions from the ioutil package. By specifying the directory name in the ioutil.ReadDir() function, it conveniently returns a list of os.FileInfo objects, as seen in the previous section.

In this example, a period symbol is used to represent the current working directory as an input to the ioutil.ReadDir() function. Then, a loop is used over a list that returns os.FileInfo objects. Finally, the loop iterates through and prints the name and the last modified timestamp by leveraging each of the os.FileInfo.Name() and os.FileInfo.ModTime() methods.

```go
package main

import (
    "fmt"
    "io/ioutil"
)

func main() {
    files, _ := ioutil.ReadDir(".")

    for _, file := range files {
        fmt.Println(file.Name(), file.ModTime())
    }
}
```

The output below is intentionally listed in lexical order. This sorting is an inherent feature of the filepath.Walk() function.

```
file1.txt 2018-10-20 14:21:11.1 -0500 EDT
file2.txt 2018-10-20 14:22:22.1 -0500 EDT
main.go   2018-10-20 14:27.33.1 -0500 EDT
```

1.5 File Tree Walk

Recursively walking a file tree from a designated starting point can be used to find and collect data or modify specific files in a directory structure. The filepath.Walk() function, from the filepath package enables this functionality. It accepts a root directory and a function to process the files and directories; symbolic links are not followed.

To demonstrate a file tree walk, the example below begins by setting up a function as a value. Then, it uses the os.FileInfo object on the os.FileInfo.IsDir() method to determine whether the entry is a directory and then prints the result, along with the respective path. Finally, the function is set as a parameter along with the root directory into the filepath.Walk() function. During execution, the initial scan function is called for each file or directory visited by the filepath.Walk() function.

```
package main

import (
    "fmt"
    "os"
    "path/filepath"
)

func main() {
    scan := func(
        path string, i os.FileInfo, _ error) error {
        fmt.Println(i.IsDir(), path)
        return nil
    }
```

```
    _ = filepath.Walk(".", scan)
}
```

Notice that the output below is intentionally sorted by file name. This is an inherent feature of the ioutil.ReadDir() function.

```
false main.go
true  dir1
false dir1/file1.txt
false dir1/file2.txt
```

2

Reading and Writing File Types

Reading and writing different file types is a critical ingredient in many programs. This chapter walks through examples that read and write the common file types found in most environments; these include Plain Text, CSV, YAML, JSON, and XML.

Several examples will take advantage of a buffer to optimize read or write operations and minimize expensive syscalls. The buffer will be used to store data until a certain size is reached before writing and retrieve more data in a single operation when reading.

This chapter will cover the following topics:

- Plain text
- CSV
- YAML
- JSON
- XML

2.1 Plain Text

Reading and writing plain text is typically done line-by-line or word-by-word. The examples in the following subchapters will demonstrate reading and writing lines of text using a native buffer.

Leveraging a buffer can be helpful when working with large files since it stores data until a certain size is reached before committing it to IO; this reduces the number of expensive system calls and other mechanics involved.

This chapter will cover the following topics:

- Reading plain text files
- Writing plain text files

2.1.1 Reading Plain Text

The bufio package Scanner is a convenient interface for reading text by lines or words from a file. The native buffer optimizes read operations by retrieving more data in a single operation. This example demonstrates reading text line-by-line from the plain text file below.

```
RTR1 1.1.1.1
RTR2 2.2.2.2
RTR3 3.3.3.3
```

To begin, the os.Open() function is used to open the above plain text file in read-only mode and then return a pointer to a value of type os.File. Next, the bufio.NewScanner() function is called with the os.File object as its parameter which returns a bufio.Scanner object that is used on the bufio.Scanner.Split() method.

Since the goal is to read each line of text, bufio.ScanLines is leveraged as an input to the bufio.Scanner.Split() method and then the Scanner advances to each new line using the bufio.Scanner.Scan() method. As each new line is advanced, each iteration is accessed from the bufio.Scanner.Text() method which is then appended to a slice and printed at the end. Finally, the os.File.Close() method is called on the os.File object to close the file and then a loop iterates through and prints each of the slice values.

```go
package main

import (
    "bufio"
    "fmt"
    "os"
)

func main() {
    file, _ := os.Open("./file.txt")

    scanner := bufio.NewScanner(file)

    scanner.Split(bufio.ScanLines)

    var lines []string

    for scanner.Scan() {
        lines = append(lines, scanner.Text())
    }
    file.Close()

    for _, line := range lines {
        fmt.Println(line)
    }
}
```

The output is displayed line-by-line as it was read from the file.

```
RTR1 1.1.1.1
RTR2 2.2.2.2
RTR3 3.3.3.3
```

2.1.2 Writing Plain Text

The bufio package provides an efficient buffered Writer that can be used to write data to a file. A buffered writer queues up bytes until a threshold is reached, then completes the write operation to minimize resources. This example walks through writing a string slice to a plain text file line-by-line.

The example below begins by defining sample data that is represented as a string slice. Each value of the sample data will be written to a new line within the file. To start, the os.OpenFile() function is used with a flag combination that creates a write-only file if none exists and appends to the file when writing. Using the os.File object that is returned from the os.OpenFile() function as input to the bufio.NewWriter() function, a new bufio.Writer object is received. Next, the slice is iterated over and each value is written to the file using the bufio.Writer.WriteString() method, while adding each new line. Finally, any remaining buffered data is written to the file with the bufio.Writer.Flush() method and the file is closed using the os.File.Close() method.

```
package main

import (
    "bufio"
    "os"
)
```

```go
func main() {
    lines := []string{"RTR1 1.1.1.1",
        "RTR2 2.2.2.2",
        "RTR3 3.3.3.3"}

    file, _ := os.OpenFile("./file.txt",
        os.O_APPEND|os.O_CREATE|os.O_WRONLY, 0644)

    writer := bufio.NewWriter(file)

    for _, line := range lines {
        _, _ = writer.WriteString(line + "\n")
    }

    writer.Flush()

    file.Close()
}
```

2.2 CSV

Comma Separated Values (CSV) is a format often used to import, export, and store data. It is also commonly used to move tabular data between incompatible formats.

The csv package supports the standard format described in RFC 4180. Each CSV file contains zero or more rows with one or more fields per row that adhere to the constraints identified below.

- Blank lines are ignored.
- White space is considered part of a field.
- Each row is seperated by a new line character.
- Carriage returns before new line characters are removed.
- New lines, spaces, and commas may be included in a quoted field.
- Quotes in quoted fields are not included unless they are quoted themselves.

This subchapter will cover the following topics:

- Reading CSV files
- Writing CSV files

2.2.1 Reading CSV

The csv package includes a NewReader() function that returns a Reader object for processing CSV records. A csv.Reader converts all \r\n sequences in its input to just \n, including multiline field values.

The CSV file below contains three columns, a header row with labels, and two rows with data. This example will demonstrate how to read a CSV file and print each of the corresponding cell values.

Here is the CSV file viewed in spreadsheet form.

HOST	IP ADDR	LOCATION
RTR1	1.1.1.1	Seattle, WA
RTR2	2.2.2.2	Nevada, NV

Below is the same CSV file as above viewed as plain text in a text editor.

```
HOST,IP ADDR,LOCATION
RTR1,1.1.1.1,"Seattle, WA"
RTR2,2.2.2.2,"Nevada, NV"
```

In this example, the file is opened in read-only mode using the os.Open() function, which returns an instance of os.File. Next, the os.File object is handed off as a parameter to the csv.NewReader() function which returns a buffered csv.Reader object. Then, the csv.Reader.Read() method is used to decode each file record into the struct and then store them in a slice until io.EOF is returned, indicating the end of the file has been reached. Finally, the slice iterates over each value.

```go
package main

import (
    "encoding/csv"
    "fmt"
    "io"
    "os"
)

type Row struct {
    ColA, ColB, ColC string
}

func main() {
    file, _ := os.Open("file.csv")

    reader := csv.NewReader(file)

    rows := []Row{}

    for {
        row, err := reader.Read()
        if err == io.EOF {
            break
        }

        rows = append(rows, Row{
            ColA: row[0], ColB: row[1], ColC: row[2],
        })
    }
    for _, row := range rows {
        fmt.Printf("%s -- %s -- %s\n",
                row.ColA, row.ColB, row.ColC)
    }
}
```

2.2.2 Writing CSV

The csv package includes a NewWriter() function which returns a Writer object that is used for writing CSV records. A csv.Writer writes records that are terminated by a newline and uses a comma as the field delimiter. This example demonstrates how to write data to a CSV file.

The example below starts by formatting the sample data in a two-dimensional slice. Then, the os.Create() function is used to create the file, truncating it if it already exists, and returning an instance of os.File object. Next, the os.File instance is used as a parameter to the csv.NewWriter() function in order to receive a buffered csv.Writer object. Then, the csv.Writer.Write() method is called to write each slice of strings to the file as CSV records. Finally, any remaining buffered data is flushed to the underlying csv.Writer using the csv.Writer.Flush() method and the file is closed with the io.File.Close() method.

```go
package main

import (
    "encoding/csv"
    "os"
)

func main() {
    rows := [][]string{
        {"HOST", "IP ADDR", "LOCATION"},
        {"RTR1", "1.1.1.1", "Seattle, WA"},
        {"RTR2", "2.2.2.2", "Nevada, NV"}}
```

```
    file, _ := os.Create("file.csv")

    writer := csv.NewWriter(file)

    for _, row := range rows {
        _ = writer.Write(row)
    }

    writer.Flush()

    file.Close()
}
```

The resulting file viewed in spreadsheet form below.

HOST	IP ADDR	LOCATION
RTR1	1.1.1.1	Seattle, WA
RTR2	2.2.2.2	Nevada, NV

The same file viewed in plain text from a text editor below.

```
HOST,IP ADDR,LOCATION
RTR1,1.1.1.1,"Seattle, WA"
RTR2,2.2.2.2,"Nevada, NV"
```

2.3 YAML

YAML Ain't Markup Language (YAML) is a popular format that is commonly used to read and write configuration files. It can also be leveraged to translate data and support compatibility.

YAML has a human-friendly layout and supports an easy to follow syntax. In general, a colon is used for key-value pairs, an indent for nesting, and a hyphen for list members.

The yaml.v2 package is compatible with most of YAML 1.1 and 1.2. It is often used as the go-to package to parse and generate YAML formatted data quickly and reliably.

This subchapter will cover the following topics:

- Reading YAML files
- Writing YAML files

2.3.1 Reading YAML

The yaml.v2 package supports an Unmarshal() function that decodes data into values from a byte slice. If the decoded values are assigned to struct fields, the field names must be exported and therefore have an upper case first letter; custom keys are defined by using "yaml" struct field tags.

In this simple example, the yaml.Unmarshal() function is used to decode the data from the YAML file below into a struct.

```
host: localhost
ports:
- 80
- 443
```

First, a struct is defined with the first letter in upper case and "yaml" field tags to identify the keys. Then, the file is read using the ioutil.ReadFile() function which returns a byte slice that is used to decode the data into a struct instance with the yaml.Unmarshal() function. Finally, the struct instance member values are printed to demonstrate the decoded YAML file.

```
package main

import (
    "fmt"
    "gopkg.in/yaml.v2"
    "io/ioutil"
)
```

```go
type Config struct {
    Host string `yaml:"host"`
    Ports []int `yaml:"ports"`
}

func main() {
    data, _ := ioutil.ReadFile("file.yaml")

    conf := Config{}

    _ = yaml.Unmarshal(data, &conf)

    fmt.Printf("%s:%d\n", conf.Host, conf.Ports)
}
```

The output below displays each value formatted on either side of a colon.

```
localhost:[80,443]
```

2.3.2 Writing YAML

The yaml.v2 package supports a Marshal() function that is used to serialized values into YAML format. While structs are typically used to support the values, maps and pointers are accepted as well. Struct fields are only serialized if they are exported and therefore have an upper case first letter. Custom keys are defined by using "yaml" struct field tags.

In this example, the yaml.Marshal() function is used to serialize data from a struct and write it to a file in YAML format. First, a struct is defined with uppercase first letters and "yaml" field tags to identify the keys in the file. Next, the struct is initialized with values and serialized using the yaml.Marshal() function. Finally, the serialized YAML formatted byte slice is received and written to a file using the ioutil.WriteFile() function.

```
package main

import (
    "gopkg.in/yaml.v2"
    "io/ioutil"
)

type Config struct {
    Host string `yaml:"host"`
    Ports []int `yaml:"ports"`
}
```

```go
func main() {
    conf := Config{
        Host: "localhost",
        Ports: []int{80,443},
    }

    data, _ := yaml.Marshal(&conf)

    _ = ioutil.WriteFile("file.yaml", data, 0644)
}
```

The output below displays the file created in the example that contains each value written in YAML format.

```yaml
host: localhost
ports:
- 80
- 443
```

2.4 JSON

JavaScript Object Notation (JSON) is a data interchange format typically used between web front-end and back-end servers and mobile applications. Most modern network appliances support a REST interface that exchanges JSON encoded data.

The json package supports reading and writing the JSON format as defined in RFC 7159.

There are a few specific Go rules that must be followed:

- Exported struct fields must start with a capital letter.
- JSON objects only support strings as keys.
- Function, channel, and complex types will not be encoded.
- Cyclic data structures are not supported.
- Pointers are dereferenced before being encoded.

This subchapter will cover the following topics:

- Reading JSON files
- Writing JSON files

2.4.1 Reading JSON

The json package has an Unmarshal() function that supports decoding data from a byte slice into values. If the decoded values are assigned to struct fields, the field names must be exported and therefore have an upper case first letter; custom keys are defined by using "json" struct field tags.

In this example, the json.Unmarshal() function is used to decode the values from the JSON formatted file below into a struct.

```
{
    "total": 3,
    "devices": [
        "SW1",
        "SW2",
        "SW3"
    ]
}
```

First, a struct is defined that aligns with the data in the JSON file. Then, "json" field tags are used to identify the individual keys. Next, the file is read with the ioutil.ReadFile() function, which returns a byte slice that is decoded into the struct instance using the json.Unmarshal() function. Finally, the struct instance member values are printed to demonstrate that the JSON file was decoded.

```
package main

import (
    "encoding/json"
```

```
    "fmt"
    "io/ioutil"
)

type Inventory struct {
    Total int `json:"total"`
    Devices []string `json:"devices"`
}

func main() {
    data, _ := ioutil.ReadFile("file.json")

    inv := Inventory{}

    _ = json.Unmarshal([]byte(data), &inv)

    fmt.Printf("Total: %d\nDevices: %q\n",
                inv.Total, inv.Devices)
}
```

The output displays each value on the right side of a colon next to the corresponding label. The devices remain in string slice format for clarity.

```
Total: 3
Devices: ["SW1" "SW2" "SW3"]
```

2.4.2 Writing JSON

The json package supports a Marshal() function that is used to serialize values into JSON format. While structs are typically used to group the values, maps are accepted as well. Struct fields are only serialized if they are exported and therefore have an upper case first letter. Custom keys are defined by using "json" struct field tags.

In this example, the json.Marshal() function is used to serialize values from a struct and write them to a file in JSON format. First, a struct is defined with an uppercase first letter and "json" field tags to identify the keys in the file. The struct values are initialized and then serialized with the json.Marshal() function. Finally, the JSON formatted byte slice is received, serialized, and then written to a file using the ioutil.WriteFile() function.

```go
package main

import (
    "encoding/json"
    "fmt"
)

type Inventory struct {
    Total int `json:"total"`
    Devices []string `json:"devices"`
}
func main() {
    data := &Inventory{
        Total: 3,
        Devices: []string{"SW1", "SW2", "SW3"},
    }
```

```go
    inv, _ := json.MarshalIndent(data, "", " ")

    fmt.Println(string(inv))
}
```

The output displays a file with each value in JSON format. While the JSON formatted data was written to a file to demonstrate the capability, it is also common to write JSON formatted data to a REST API, as shown later in Chapter 4.2.

```json
{
    "total": 3,
    "devices": [
        "SW1",
        "SW2",
        "SW3"
    ]
}
```

2.5 XML

Extensible Markup Language (XML) is a markup language commonly used as a data communication format in web services. The streamlined format is often preferred over JSON due to its compact structure.

The xml package supports reading and writing XML 1.0. Since XML forms a tree data structure, it can be define in a similar hierarchy using structs in Go. The examples in the subchapters that follow will leverage structs to encode and decode XML.

This subchapter will cover the following topics:
- Reading XML files
- Writing XML files

2.5.1 Reading XML

The xml package has an Unmarshal() function that supports decoding data from a byte slice into values. If the decoded values are assigned to struct fields, the field names must be exported and therefore have an upper case first letter; custom keys are defined by using "xml" struct field tags.

In this example, the xml.Unmarshal() function is used to decode the values from the XML formatted file below into a struct.

```
<campus name="campus1">
    <!-- building-comment -->
    <building name="bldg1">
        <!-- device-comment -->
        <device type="router" name="rtr1"></device>
    </building>
</campus>
```

First, a struct is defined and "xml" field tags are used to identify the keys in the file. Next, the file is read with the ioutil.ReadFile() function and a byte slice is returned, which is then decoded into a struct instance with the xml.Unmarshal() function. Finally, the struct instance member values are printed to demonstrate the decoded data.

```
package main

import (
    "encoding/xml"
    "fmt"
```

```go
        "io/ioutil"
)
type Campus struct {
    XMLName xml.Name `xml:"campus"`
    Name string `xml:"name,attr"`
    Comment string `xml:",comment"`
    Building Building
}
type Building struct {
    XMLName xml.Name `xml:"building"`
    Name string `xml:"name,attr"`
    Comment string `xml:",comment"`
    Device Device
}
type Device struct {
    XMLName xml.Name `xml:"device"`
    Name string `xml:"name,attr"`
    Type string `xml:"type,attr"`
}

func main() {
    data, _ := ioutil.ReadFile("file.xml")

    camp := &Campus{}

    _ = xml.Unmarshal([]byte(data), &camp)

    fl := fmt.Println
    fl("Campus Name: ", camp.Name)
    fl("Building Name: ", camp.Building.Name)
    fl("Building Comment:", camp.Comment)
    fl("Device Comment: ", camp.Building.Comment)
    fl("Device Name: ", camp.Building.Device.Name)
    fl("Device Type: ", camp.Building.Device.Type)
}
```

The output displays each value after its respective field name.

```
Campus Name: campus1
Building Name: bldg1
Building Comment: building-comment
Device Comment: device-comment
Device Name: rtr1
Device Type: router
```

2.5.2 Writing XML

The xml package supports the Marshal() function that is used to serialized values into XML format. While structs are typically used to group the values, maps are accepted as well. Struct fields are only serialized if they are exported and therefore have an upper case first letter. Custom keys are defined by using "xml" struct field tags.

In this example, the xml.Marshal() function is used to serialize values from a struct and write them to a file in XML format. First, a struct is defined with an uppercase first letter and "xml" field tags are used to identify the keys. The struct values are initialized and then serialize with the xml.Marshal() function. Finally, the serialized XML formatted byte slice is received and then written to a file using the ioutil.WriteFile() function.

```go
package main

import (
    "encoding/xml"
    "io/ioutil"
)

type Campus struct {
    XMLName xml.Name `xml:"campus"`
    Name string `xml:"name,attr"`
    Comment string `xml:",comment"`
    Building Building
}
```

```
type Building struct {
    XMLName xml.Name `xml:"building"`
    Name string `xml:"name,attr"`
    Comment string `xml:",comment"`
    Device Device
}
type Device struct {
    XMLName xml.Name `xml:"device"`
    Name string `xml:"name,attr"`
    Type string `xml:"type,attr"`
}

func main() {
    camp := &Campus{Name: "campus1",
        Comment: "building-comment",
        Building: Building{Name: "bldg1",
            Comment: "device-comment",
            Device: Device{Name: "rtr1",
                Type: "router"}}}

    indt, _ := xml.MarshalIndent(camp, "", "    ")

    _ = ioutil.WriteFile("file.xml", indt, 0644)
}
```

The output displays the file with each value in XML format. While the XML was written to a file to demonstrate the process, it is also common to write XML to a REST API.

```
<campus name="campus1">
    <!-- building-comment -->
    <building name="bldg1">
        <!-- device-comment -->
        <device type="router" name="rtr1"></device>
    </building>
</campus>
```

3

Text Templates

Text templates are often used in network operations to generate a large number of configurations that consistently adhere to a standard template. They enable consistent accuracy and allow for revision control.

The template package handles templates by parsing text and evaluating dynamic elements. This chapter looks at common template actions and then introduces a basic template before going into template inheritance.

This chapter will cover the following topics:

- Defining template elements
- Creating a basic template
- Implementing template inheritance

3.1 Template Elements

The building blocks of a template are its elements. Elements consist of arguments and actions that are surrounded by double curly braces. Arguments include values and actions, which are composed of statements, such as if-else, range or with.

Element	Description
{{.}}	Root element
{{.Var}}	Variable
{{.Var}}	Remove whitespace on either side
{{ $version := "0.1"}} {{ $version }}	Internal variable assignment
{{/* comment here */}}	Comment
Name: {{if .Name }} {{ .Name }} {{ else }} anonymous {{end}}.	If-else conditional
{{with .Var}} {{end}}	With statement
{{range .Array}} {{end}}	Range over slice, map or channel
{{ lt 3 4 }}	Less than (other boolean operators: eq, ne, lt, le, gt, ge)

3.2 Basic Template

A basic template consists of a data source and a single template. Template inheritance, which is covered in the next section, is used to piece together nested templates.

In this example, three files are used, a CSV data file, a template file, and a Go file. The CSV data file below represents a list of VLANs, one per row with numbers in the first column and names in the second. The template file will represent the format to configure each VLAN. It will iterate over each row of the data file and format the data from both columns in the respective layout. The Go file will be used to merge the CSV and template files together then generate an output.

```
1,ONE
2,TWO
3,THREE
```

Now that the CSV data file is defined above, the template file is used to position the data. The template file, defined below, uses the range element to encapsulate the middle two lines. It iterates over the root element slice struct of data that represents the rows in the CSV data file. Within the loop, the plain text is followed by a variable that is used to apply the struct member. Take note of the dash element that is used to trim the whitespace after the name in the template file below.

```
{{range .}}
vlan {{ .Id }}
name {{ .Name -}}
{{end}}
```

Walking through the Go file below, the CSV data file is opened in read-only mode with the os.Open() function, returning an instance of os.File. Next, the os.File instance is handed off as a parameter to the csv.NewReader() function in order to receive a buffered csv.Reader object. Then, a slice instance of the Vlans struct is created that is used to store the values from each row of the CSV file. The csv.Reader.Read() method is used to decode the file line-by-line into the struct fields. It then stores them in a slice until the expected io.EOF error is returned, indicating the end of the file has been reached. Finally, the template file is parsed with the template.ParseFiles() function and then merged together with the template file by calling the tmpl.Execute() function, sending the result to the terminal standard output.

```
package main

import (
    "encoding/csv"
    "io"
    "os"
    "text/template"
)

type Vlans struct {
    Id, Name string
}

func main() {
    data, _ := os.Open("file.csv")

    reader := csv.NewReader(data)

    vlans := []Vlans{}

    for {
        row, err := reader.Read()
        if err == io.EOF {
            break
        }
```

```
        vlans = append(vlans, Vlans{
            Id: row[0],
            Name: row[1],
        })
    }
    tmpl, _ := template.ParseFiles("file.tmpl")

    _ = tmpl.Execute(os.Stdout, vlans)
}
```

The output demonstrates the basic template data.

```
vlan 1
  name ONE
vlan 2
  name TWO
vlan 3
  name THREE
```

3.3 Template Inheritance

Template inheritance is used to work with nested templates by building a base skeleton that contains child templates. This enables the ability to reuse child templates across multiple base templates. Imagine multiple types of router templates, all sharing the same common child BGP or NTP template.

In this example, template inheritance is used to piece together a router configuration that consists of base configuration data and multiple child components that represent a router BGP and NTP configuration. The data source will be set in the YAML file below to easily parse the user input.

```
base:
  hostname: router1

bgp:
  as: 1234
  id: 4.4.4.4
  neighbors:
  - ip: 1.1.1.1
    as: 1
  - ip: 2.2.2.2
    as: 2

ntp:
  source: Loopback0
  primary: 11.11.11.11
  secondary: 22.22.22.22
```

Three template files will be used in total, a base template and two nested templates. In each file, the comment element is leveraged at the top to identify the file name and also the define element to assign the template name. Since this is template inheritance, the child templates are associated to the base by referencing the child template name along with the template element in the respective position.

```
{{/* base.tmpl */}}

{{define "base"}}
hostname {{.Base.Hostname}}
{{template "bgp" .}}
{{template "ntp" .}}
{{end}}
```

```
{{/* bgp.tmpl */}}

{{ define "bgp" }}
router {{ .Bgp.As }}
router-id {{ .Bgp.Id -}}
{{range .Bgp.Neighbors}}
neighbor {{ .Ip }} remote-as {{ .As -}}
{{end}}
{{ end }}
```

```
{{/* ntp.tmpl */}}

{{ define "ntp" }}
ntp source-interface {{.Ntp.Source}}
ntp server {{.Ntp.Primary}} prefer
ntp server {{.Ntp.Secondary}}
{{ end }}
```

In the Go file below, the YAML file is read into a byte slice using the ioutil.ReadFile() function. Then the yaml.Unmarshal() function is used to parse the byte slice into the struct instance. Next, a map of the templates is created by parsing the base and child templates. Finally, the data is merged with the template map using the template.Template.ExecuteTemplate() method to send the data to the terminal standard output.

```go
package main

import (
    "text/template"
    "os"
    "gopkg.in/yaml.v2"
    "io/ioutil"
)
type Config struct {
    Base Base `base`
    Bgp Bgp `bgp`
    Ntp Ntp `ntp`
}
type Base struct {
    Hostname string `hostname`
}
type Bgp struct {
    As string `as`
    Id string `id`
    Neighbors []Neighbors `neighbors`
}
type Neighbors struct {
    Ip string `ip`
    As string `as`
}
type Ntp struct {
    Source string `source `
    Primary string `primary`
    Secondary string `secondary`
}

func main() {
    config := Config{}

    data, _ := ioutil.ReadFile("file.yaml")

    _ = yaml.Unmarshal(data, &config)

    tmpl := make(map[string]*template.Template)

    files, _ := template.ParseFiles("base.tmpl",
        "bgp.tmpl", "ntp.tmpl")

    tmpl["base.tmpl"] = template.Must(files, nil)

    _ = tmpl["base.tmpl"].ExecuteTemplate(
        os.Stdout, "base", config)
}
```

The output below shows the combined data and templates.

```
hostname router1

router 1234
  router-id 4.4.4.4
  neighbor 1.1.1.1 remote-as 1
  neighbor 2.2.2.2 remote-as 2

ntp source-interface Loopback0
ntp server 11.11.11.11 prefer
ntp server 22.22.22.22
```

4

HTTP Client

A Hypertext Transfer Protocol (HTTP) client is used to establish a connection and request data from an HTTP server. The most common methods are GET and POST. The http package supports attributes, such as timeouts, redirects, and cookies, as defined in RFC 2616. While this package has more basic methods, such as the http.Client.Get() and http.Client.Post() methods, in order to apply custom headers the http.NewRequest() function can be used together with the http.Client.Do() method. This chapter demonstrates the GET and POST requests by walking through examples using the more common features, such as client timeouts, cookies, and custom headers.

This chapter will cover the following HTTP client topics:

- GET request
- POST request

4.1 GET

The http package supports the GET method as defined in RFC 7231, section 4.3.1. A simple GET request can be done with the http.Client.Get() method or, if custom headers are needed, a combination of the http.NewRequest() function and the http.Client.Do() method can be used.

In this example, the method, URL, and body are setup using the http.NewRequest() function in order to receive an http.Request object. Then, a header is set with the http.Request.Header.Set() method using standard key-value pair as input. Next, the Timeout field is initialized in the http.Client struct which returns a new http.Client object. Now that the GET request is built with the URL, and the client header is defined, they are used together with the custom timeout to send and receive the HTTP request using the http.Client.Do() method. Finally, the Response object is received from the http.Client.Do() method and the request body is closed prior to printing the response.

```
package main

import (
    "fmt"
    "io/ioutil"
    "net/http"
    "time"
)
```

```go
func main() {
    req, _ := http.NewRequest("GET", "http://example.com", nil)

    req.Header.Set("Cache-Control", "no-cache")

    client := &http.Client{Timeout: time.Second * 10}

    resp, _ := client.Do(req)

    body, _ := ioutil.ReadAll(resp.Body)

    resp.Body.Close()

    fmt.Printf("%s\n", body)
}
```

4.2 POST

The http package supports the POST method as defined in RFC 7231, section 4.3.3. A simple POST request can be done with the http.Client.Post() method. If custom headers are needed, a combination of the http.NewRequest() function and the http.Client.Do() method can be used.

In this example, the method, URL, and body are defined using the http.NewRequest() function in order to receive an http.Request object. Then, the header is set with the http.Request.Header.Set() method using standard key-value pair as input. Next, the cookie Name and Value fields are defined in the http.Cookie struct, which returns a new Cookie object that is added to the request with the http.Request.AddCookie() method. Next, the Timeout field is set in the http.Client struct and then a new http.Client object is returned. Now that the POST request is built and the header is set, they are used together with the new client to send and receive the HTTP request in the http.Client.Do() method. Finally, the Response object is returned from the http.Client.Do() method and the request body is closed prior to printing the response.

```
package main

import (
    "bytes"
    "fmt"
    "io/ioutil"
    "net/http"
    "time"
)
```

```go
func main() {
    url := "http://example.com"

    data := []byte(`{"hello": "world"}`)

    req, _ := http.NewRequest("POST", url, bytes.NewBuffer(data))

    req.Header.Set("Content-Type", "application/json")

    cookie := http.Cookie{Name: "cookiename", Value: "cookievalue"}

    req.AddCookie(&cookie)

    client := &http.Client{Timeout: time.Second * 10}

    resp, _ := client.Do(req)

    body, _ := ioutil.ReadAll(resp.Body)

    resp.Body.Close()

    fmt.Printf("%s\n", body)
}
```

5

SSH Client

Secure Shell (SSH) is commonly used to execute commands on remote servers. It can also be used to transfer files with Secure File Transfer Protocol (SFTP). While the ssh package is not native to the Go standard library, it is the official SSH package written and supported by the Go team. The ssh package supports several methods for authenticating, such as using a password or private key. This chapter will cover both forms of authentication by walking through examples that demonstrate executing commands and transferring files.

This chapter will cover the following SSH client topics:

- Single command with private key authentication
- Multiple commands with password authentication
- SFTP file copy with password authentication

5.1 Single Command with Private Key Authentication

The ssh package supports private key authentication. This form of authentication is more secure than a simple password because it is difficult to brute force and eliminates the need to remember or write down a password.

To prepare for this example, the public and private keys are generated on the local machine using the ssh-keygen utility. Ssh-keygen is available on most Linux or Mac installations. This utility creates a public (id_rsa.pub) and private key file (id_rsa) as shown below.

```
$ ssh-keygen -b 4096
Generating public/private rsa key pair.
Enter file in which to save the key (/Users/username/.ssh/id_rsa):
Enter passphrase (empty for no passphrase):
Enter same passphrase again:
Your identification has been saved in /Users/username/.ssh/id_rsa.
Your public key has been saved in /Users/username/.ssh/id_rsa.pub.
The key fingerprint is:
SHA256:2Bx44Vo8c6l...BeawUlC+z9l9UW5F username@mycomputer.local
The key's randomart image is:
+---[RSA 4096]----+
|        o.@=...ooo|
|       o.*+@+   oO|
|       ..=..*=   oB|
|       . o+.=o&  Eo|
|        + To.+.=. |
|        o   .o    |
+----[SHA256]-----+
```

Next, the public key (id_rsa.pub) is copied over to the remote host using the ssh-copy-id tool. It will be placed inside the ~/.ssh/authorized_keys file on that host.

```
$ ssh-copy-id remotehost

/usr/bin/ssh-copy-id: INFO: Source of key(s) to be installed:
"/Users/username/.ssh/id_rsa.pub"
/usr/bin/ssh-copy-id: INFO: attempting to log in with the new
key(s), to filter out any that are already installed
/usr/bin/ssh-copy-id: INFO: 1 key(s) remain to be installed -- if
you are prompted now it is to install the new keys

Password:

Number of key(s) added: 1

Now try logging into the machine, with: "ssh 'remotehost'"
and check to make sure that only the key(s) you wanted were added.
```

Now that the public key is on the remote host and the private key is in place locally, both keys are properly staged for private key authentication.

Next, to prepare to validate the identity of the remote host, the remote host public key is obtained as a fingerprint in known_hosts file format using the ssh-keyscan utility. The fingerprint may already be present in the local ~/.ssh/known_hosts file if the local machine has previously connected to the host via SSH.

```
$ ssh-keyscan remotehost
# remotehost:22 SSH-2.0-OpenSSH_7.6
remotehost ecdsa-sha2-nistp256 AAAAE...jZHN
```

This example now begins by copying the remote host public key into a variable that will be used to verify the remote host and prevent spoofing in the client configuration. Using the ssh.ParseKnownHosts() function, the public key is parsed in known_hosts file format. The key is hardcoded for simplicity sake; however, in practice, it may be parse from a file or database.

Next, the private key file is read with the ioutil.ReadFile() function and is returned as a byte slice. It is then used together with the passphrase in the ssh.ParsePrivateKeyWithPassphrase() function to obtain a Signer instance. Then, the ssh.ClientConfig struct is built by adding the username and then the Signer signature into the ssh.PublicKeys() function for authentication. Next, the HostKeyCallback is defined with the ssh.FixedHostKey() function for authorization. Finally, the maximum amount of time for the TCP connection to establish is set as the Timeout value, where zero means no timeout.

Note that the option to bypass remote host authorization is available by replacing the ssh.FixedHostKey() function with the ssh.InsecureIgnoreHostKey() function, however, this insecure function is only recommended in a non-production lab environment.

While not covered in this example, a list of acceptable key types and ciphers could optionally be defined along with an order of preference in the ssh.ClientConfig struct. The key types identified by KeyAlgoXxxx constants would be defined as values in the HostKeyAlgorithms slice. The acceptable cipher list would be defined in the Cipher field in the ssh.Config struct that is embedded in the ssh.ClientConfig struct. Additionally, legacy CBC mode ciphers may be added as well.

Now that the ssh.ClientConfig struct is built, it is used together with the remote host to start the SSH connection by using the ssh.Dial() function to return a ssh.Client instance. Next, a new session is created with the ssh.Client.NewSession() method which is then mapped to the terminal's local standard output and error for demonstration purpose. Finally, the command is ran on the remote host by using the ssh.Session.Run() function and then calling the ssh.Session.Close() method to terminate the connection.

```go
package main

import (
    "golang.org/x/crypto/ssh"
    "io/ioutil"
    "os"
    "time"
```

```go
)

func main() {
    user := "username"
    pass := []byte("password")
    remotehost := "remotehost:22"
    cmd := "hostname"
    privkeyfile := "/Users/username/.ssh/id_rsa"
    knownhost := []byte("remotehost ecdsa-sha2-nistp256 AAE...jZHN")

    _, _, hostkey, _, _, _ := ssh.ParseKnownHosts(knownhost)

    privkeydata, _ := ioutil.ReadFile(privkeyfile)

    parsekey := ssh.ParsePrivateKeyWithPassphrase
    privkey, _ := parsekey(privkeydata, pass)

    config := &ssh.ClientConfig{
        User: user,
        Auth: []ssh.AuthMethod{
            ssh.PublicKeys(privkey),
        },
        HostKeyCallback: ssh.FixedHostKey(hostkey),
        Timeout: 5 * time.Second,
    }
    conn, _ := ssh.Dial("tcp", remotehost, config)

    sess, _ := conn.NewSession()

    sess.Stdout = os.Stdout
    sess.Stderr = os.Stderr

    _ = sess.Run(cmd)

    sess.Close()
}
```

5.2: Multiple Commands with Password Authentication

This next example starts out by gathering the remote host public key that will be used to validate the identity of the remote host and build the client configuration.

As with the previous example, the remote host public key is obtained as a fingerprint in known_hosts file format using the ssh-keyscan utility. Again, it may also be present in the local ~/.ssh/known_hosts file if the local machine has previously connected to the host via SSH.

```
$ ssh-keyscan remotehost
# remotehost:22 SSH-2.0-OpenSSH_7.6
remotehost ecdsa-sha2-nistp256 AAAAE...jZHN
```

Next, the remote host public key is copied into a variable that is used to prevent spoofing in the client configuration. Then, the public key is parsed in known_hosts file format using the ssh.ParseKnownHosts() function. While the key is hardcoded for simplicity sake, it may be parsed from a file or database in practice. Likewise, while the username and password are hardcoded in this example, they should be retrieved using more secure and convenient means in a production environment. Next, the ssh.ClientConfig struct is built by adding the username and then the password into the ssh.Password() function for authentication. Authorization is enabled by defining the HostKeyCallback with the ssh.FixedHostKey() function. Finally, the maximum amount of time for the TCP connection to establish is set as the Timeout value, where zero means no timeout.

Note that the option to bypass remote host authorization is available by replacing the ssh.FixedHostKey() function with ssh.InsecureIgnoreHostKey() function, however, this insecure function is only recommended in a non-production lab environment.

While not covered in this example, a list of acceptable key types and ciphers could optionally be defined along with an order of preference in the ssh.ClientConfig struct. The key types identified by KeyAlgoXxxx constants would be defined as values in the HostKeyAlgorithms slice. The acceptable cipher list would be defined in the Cipher field in the ssh.Config struct that is embedded in the ssh.ClientConfig struct. Additionally, legacy CBC mode ciphers may be added as well.

Now that the ssh.ClientConfig struct has been built, it is used together with the remote host to start the SSH connection by using the ssh.Dial() function to return the ssh.Client instance. Next, a new session is created with the ssh.Client.NewSession() method and then is mapped to the terminal's local standard error and output for demonstration purpose. Then, a shell is started on the remote host using the ssh.Session.Shell() method to run the commands in. Finally, the commands are ran and then the ssh.Session.Wait() method is used to wait until the commands execute prior to calling the ssh.Session.Close() method to close the session and terminate the connection.

```
package main

import (
    "fmt"
    "golang.org/x/crypto/ssh"
    "os"
    "time"
)

func main() {
    user := "username"
    pass := "password"
    remotehost:= "remotehost:22"
    knownhost := []byte("remotehost ecdsa-sha2-nistp256 AAE...jZHN")
```

```go
    _, _, hostkey, _, _, _ := ssh.ParseKnownHosts(knownhost)

    config := &ssh.ClientConfig{
        User: user,
        Auth: []ssh.AuthMethod{
            ssh.Password(pass),
        },
        HostKeyCallback: ssh.FixedHostKey(hostkey),
        Timeout: 5 * time.Second,
    }
    conn, _ := ssh.Dial("tcp", remotehost, config)

    sess, _ := conn.NewSession()

    stdin, _ := sess.StdinPipe()

    sess.Stdout = os.Stdout
    sess.Stderr = os.Stderr

    _ = sess.Shell()

    fmt.Fprintf(stdin,"%s\n%s\n%s\n","pwd", "ls", "exit")

    _ = sess.Wait()

    sess.Close()
}
```

5.3: SFTP File Copy with Password Authentication

In this SFTP example, the remote host public key is retrieved to validate the identity of the remote host. It will be used to build the client configuration.

First, the remote host public key is collected as a fingerprint in known_hosts file format using the ssh-keyscan utility. Again, it may also be seen in the local ~/.ssh/known_hosts file if the local machine has previously connected to the host via SSH.

```
$ ssh-keyscan remotehost
# remotehost:22 SSH-2.0-OpenSSH_7.6
remotehost ecdsa-sha2-nistp256 AAAAE...jZHN
```

Next, the remote host public key is copied into a variable that is used to prevent spoofing in the client configuration. Then, the public key is parsed from the entry in known_hosts file format using the ssh.ParseKnownHosts() function. The key is hardcoded for simplicity sake; however, in practice, it may be parsed from a file or database. Next, the ssh.ClientConfig struct is built by adding the username and password into the ssh.Password() function for authentication. Then, the HostKeyCallback is defined with the ssh.FixedHostKey() function for authorization. Finally, the maximum amount of time for the TCP connection to establish is set in Timeout, where a value of zero means no timeout.

Note that it is possible to bypass remote host authorization by replacing the ssh.FixedHostKey() function with the ssh.InsecureIgnoreHostKey() function, however, this insecure function is only recommended in a non-production lab environment.

While not covered in this example, a list of acceptable key types and ciphers could optionally be defined along with an order of preference in the ssh.ClientConfig struct. The key types identified by KeyAlgoXxxx constants would be defined as values in the HostKeyAlgorithms slice. The acceptable cipher list would be defined in the Cipher field in the ssh.Config struct that is embedded in the ssh.ClientConfig struct. Additionally, legacy CBC mode ciphers may be added as well.

Now that the ssh.ClientConfig struct is built, it is used together with the remote host to start the SSH connection by using the ssh.Dial() function to return the ssh.Client instance.

Next, a new SFTP client is created by calling the sftp.NewClient() function and using the ssh.Client session object as a parameter. This allows the sftp.Client.MkdirAll() method to create a directory that includes all parents in the path and the sftp.Client.Create() method to stage the file that it will be copied to. Now that the target directory and file are created, the source file is opened with the os.Open() function and the io.Copy() function is used to copy it until EOF is reached on the source. Then, the sftp.File.Close() method is called on the destination file and the SFTP session is closed with the sftp.Client.Close() method. Finally the SSH session is closed using the ssh.Client.Close() method.

```
package main

import (
    "github.com/pkg/sftp"
    "golang.org/x/crypto/ssh"
    "io"
    "os"
    "time"
)
```

```go
func main() {
    user := "username"
    pass := "password"
    remotehost:= "remotehost:22"
    knownhost := []byte("remotehost ecdsa-sha2-nistp256 AAE...jZHN")

    _, _, hostkey, _, _, _ := ssh.ParseKnownHosts(knownhost)

    config := &ssh.ClientConfig{
        User: user,
        Auth: []ssh.AuthMethod{
            ssh.Password(pass),
        },
        HostKeyCallback: ssh.FixedHostKey(hostkey),
        Timeout: 5 * time.Second,
    }
    conn, _ := ssh.Dial("tcp", remotehost, config)

    client, _ := sftp.NewClient(conn)

    _ = client.MkdirAll("./dir")

    dstfile, _ := client.Create("./dir/dest.txt")

    srcfile, _ := os.Open("./src.txt")

    _, _ = io.Copy(dstfile, srcfile)

    dstfile.Close()
    client.Close()
    conn.Close()
}
```

6

IP Address Manipulation

IP address manipulation is used to efficiently parse and process IP addresses and their respective network masks. The net package provides methods for working with IP addresses and CIDR notation that conform to RFC 4632 and RFC 4291. This chapter will cover common tasks associated with manipulating IP addresses, such as listing all IPs within a network, determining whether an IP is contained within a network, and converting masks between CIDR and dot-decimal notation.

This chapter will cover the following topics:

- Determining whether a network contains an IP
- Listing all IPs within a network
- Converting between network mask formats

6.1: Network Contains IP

This example will define a CIDR network and slice with two IP addresses, one inside the CIDR network and one outside. It will loop through each IP in the slice to determine whether it is contained within the network.

The example starts by using the net.ParseCIDR() function on a CIDR network address in string format to return a net.IPNet object. Next, it uses the net.ParseIP() function to return a net.IP object from the string address. Finally, the net.IP object is used as a parameter in the net.IPNet.Contains() method on the CIDR network to retrieve and print the result.

```
package main

import (
    "fmt"
    "net"
)

func main() {
    netw := "1.1.1.0/24"
    ips := []string{"1.1.1.1", "2.2.2.2"}

    for _, ip := range ips {
        _, cidrnet, _ := net.ParseCIDR(netw)

        addr := net.ParseIP(ip)

        result := cidrnet.Contains(addr)
```

```
        fmt.Printf("%s contains %s: %t \n", cidrnet, addr, result)
    }
}
```

The output below displays whether the IP is contained within the CIDR network.

```
1.1.1.0/24 contains 1.1.1.1: true
1.1.1.0/24 contains 2.2.2.2: false
```

6.2: List Network IPs

This example demonstrates how to list all IP addresses within a network, including the network and broadcast. To start, the net.ParseCIDR() function is used on the CIDR address in string format to return a net.IP and net.IPNet object. Next, a function is defined as a value that is used later to increment in the loop statement. This function accepts a net.IP byte-slice parameter that initializes the starting value of the loop and ultimately increments the respective octet value.

Next, a final loop is defined that iterates through the network IPs. First, the net.IP value is initialized by using the net.IP.Mask() method to retrieve the starting network address. Then, the net.IPNet.Contains() method is put in place as the terminating condition to end the loop. Finally, the increment function is used to walk through the respective network.

```
package main

import (
    "fmt"
    "net"
)

func main() {
    netw := "1.1.1.1/30"
    ip, ipnet, _ := net.ParseCIDR(netw)
```

```go
inc := func(ip net.IP) {

    for i := len(ip) - 1; i >= 0; i-- {
        ip[i]++
        if ip[i] >= 1 {
            break
        }
    }
}

ipmask := ip.Mask(ipnet.Mask)

for ip := ipmask; ipnet.Contains(ip); inc(ip) {
    fmt.Println(ip)
}
}
```

The output below displays whether the IP is contained within the CIDR network.

```
1.1.1.0
1.1.1.1
1.1.1.2
1.1.1.3
```

6. 3: Mask Conversion

This example will convert an IPv4 mask from slash notation to dot-decimal notation, then from dot-decimal back to IPv4 slash notation.

To start, the net.ParseCIDR() function is used on the CIDR address in string format to return a net.IP and net.IPNet object. Then, to convert the mask, the net.IPNet.Mask byte-slice is assigned to a variable and then each index is formatted into the dot-decimal mask string and printed.

Next, to convert the mask back to slash notation, the dot-decimal mask is fed into the net.ParseIP() function to return a net.IP object. The net.IP object is implemented on the net.IP.To4() method to convert the IP back to a 4-byte representation. This net.IP object is enclosed in the net.IPMask() function to return a net.IPMask object. Finally, the net.IPMask.Size() method is used to return the mask length, or the number of leading ones in the mask.

```go
package main

import (
    "fmt"
    "net"
)

func main() {
    netw := "1.1.1.1/27"
    ipv4IP, ipv4Net, _ := net.ParseCIDR(netw)

    m := ipv4Net.Mask
```

```go
    dotmask := fmt.Sprintf("%d.%d.%d.%d",
        m[0], m[1], m[2], m[3])

    fmt.Printf("Dot-decimal notation: %s %s",
        ipv4IP, dotmask)

    cidrmask := net.IPMask(
        net.ParseIP(dotmask).To4())

    length, _ := cidrmask.Size()

    slash := fmt.Sprintf("%s/%d", ipv4IP, length)

    fmt.Println("\nCIDR notation: ", slash)
}
```

The output below displays the IP with the dot-decimal mask followed by the CIDR mask representation.

```
Dot-decimal notation: 1.1.1.1 255.255.255.224
CIDR notation: 1.1.1.1/27
```

7

DNS Record Lookup

DNS record lookup is enabled by domain name resolution. The net package includes methods to look up the more common DNS records. This chapter covers those methods and how to use them to look up records that include forward, reverse, CNAME, MX, NS, SRV, and TXT.

This chapter will cover the following DNS record lookups:

- Forward (A)
- Reverse (PTR)
- Canonical Name (CNAME)
- Mail Exchanger (MX)
- Name Servers (NS)
- Service (SRV)
- Text (TXT)

7.1: Forward (A)

The net.LookupIP() function accepts a string and returns a slice of net.IP objects that represent that host's IPv4 and/or IPv6 addresses.

```
package main

import (
    "fmt"
    "net"
)

func main() {
    ips, _ := net.LookupIP("google.com")

    for _, ip := range ips {
        fmt.Println(ip.String())
    }
}
```

The output below lists the A records for google.com that were returned in both IPv4 and IPv6 formats.

```
172.217.1.238
2607:f8b0:4000:80e::200e
```

7.2: Reverse (PTR)

The net.LookupAddr() function performs a reverse lookup for the address and returns a list of names that map to the address. Be aware that the host C library resolver will only return one result. To bypass the host resolver, a custom resolver must be used.

```
package main

import (
    "fmt"
    "net"
)

func main() {
    names, _ := net.LookupAddr("8.8.8.8")

    for _, name := range names {
        fmt.Println(name)
    }
}
```

The single reverse record that was returned for the address is shown below, including the trailing period symbol at the end.

```
google-public-dns-a.google.com.
```

7. 3: Canonical Name (CNAME)

The net.LookupCNAME() function accepts a hostname as a string and returns a single canonical name for the provided host.

```
package main

import (
    "fmt"
    "net"
)

func main() {
    cname, _ := net.LookupCNAME(
        "research.swtch.com")

    fmt.Println(cname)
}
```

The CNAME record that was returned for the research.swtch.com domain is shown below, including the trailing period symbol at the end.

```
ghs.google.com.
```

7. 4: Mail Exchanger (MX)

The net.LookupMX() function accepts a domain name as a string and returns a slice of MX structs sorted by preference. An MX struct is made up of a Host as a string and Pref as a uint16.

```
package main

import (
    "fmt"
    "net"
)

func main() {
    mxs, _ := net.LookupMX("google.com")

    for _, mx := range mxs {
        fmt.Println(mx.Host, mx.Pref)
    }
}
```

The output lists each MX record for the domain followed by each respective preference.

```
aspmx.l.google.com. 10
alt1.aspmx.l.google.com. 20
alt2.aspmx.l.google.com. 30
alt3.aspmx.l.google.com. 40
alt4.aspmx.l.google.com. 50
```

7. 5: Name Servers (NS)

The net.LookupNS() function accepts a domain name as a string and returns DNS NS records as a slice of NS structs. An NS struct is made up of a Host as a string.

```go
package main

import (
    "fmt"
    "net"
)

func main() {
    nss, _ := net.LookupNS("gmail.com")

    for _, ns := range nss {
        fmt.Println(ns.Host)
    }
}
```

The NS records that support the domain are shown below, including the trailing period symbol at the end.

```
ns1.google.com.
ns4.google.com.
ns3.google.com.
ns2.google.com.
```

7. 6: Service (SRV)

The net.LookupSRV() function accepts a service, protocol, and domain name as a string. It returns a canonical name as a string along with a slice of SRV structs. An SRV struct supports a Target as a string and Port, Priority, and Weight as uint16's. The net.LookupSRV() function attempts to resolve an SRV query of the service, protocol, and domain name, sorted by priority and randomized by weight within a priority.

```go
package main

import (
    "fmt"
    "net"
)

func main() {
    cname, srvs, _ := net.LookupSRV(
        "xmpp-server", "tcp", "google.com")

    fmt.Printf("\ncname: %s \n\n", cname)

    for _, srv := range srvs {
        fmt.Printf("%v:%v:%d:%d\n",
            srv.Target, srv.Port,
            srv.Priority, srv.Weight)
    }
}
```

The output below demonstrates the CNAME return, followed by the respective SRV record target, port, priority, and weight separated by a colon.

```
cname: _xmpp-server._tcp.google.com.

xmpp-server.l.google.com.:5269:5:0
alt2.xmpp-server.l.google.com.:5269:20:0
alt1.xmpp-server.l.google.com.:5269:20:0
alt3.xmpp-server.l.google.com.:5269:20:0
alt4.xmpp-server.l.google.com.:5269:20:0
```

7. 7: Text (TXT)

The net.LookupTXT() function accepts a domain name as a string
and returns a list of DNS TXT records as a slice of strings.

```
package main

import (
    "fmt"
    "net"
)

func main() {
    txts, _ := net.LookupTXT("gmail.com")

    for _, txt := range txts {
        fmt.Println(txt)
    }
}
```

The single TXT record for gmail.com is shown below.

```
v=spf1 redirect=_spf.google.com
```

8

Regex Pattern Matching

Regular expression pattern matching is used to match a sequence of characters that are defined by a search pattern. The regexp package leverages the fast and thread-safe RE2 regular expression engine. While it does not support backtracking, it does guarantee linear time execution. This chapter covers simple matching, match groups, named matches, template expansion, and multi-line split.

This chapter will cover the following regex pattern topics:

- Simple matching
- Match groups
- Named capture groups
- Template expansion
- Multi-line delimited split

8.1: Simple Matching

Simple pattern matching covers the basic concept of returning a result from processing a regular expression pattern against a data set. In this example, the data set is first identified and then the regexp.MustCompile() function is used to define the pattern. The pattern leverages the \w+ syntax to match one or more word characters on either side of the dot. Then, using the dataset as input, the regexp.Regexp.FindString() method is called on the pattern to return the result. If multiple string matches were needed from the pattern, the regexp.Regexp.FindAllString() method would have been used and a slice returned.

```go
package main

import (
    "fmt"
    "regexp"
)

func main() {
    data := `# host.domain.tld #`

    pattern := regexp.MustCompile(`\w+.\w+.\w+`)

    result := pattern.FindString(data)

    fmt.Println(result)
}
```

The simple match using the \w+.\w+.\w+ pattern against the data set is shown below.

```
host.domain.tld
```

8.2: Match Groups

Using parentheses in the search pattern identifies individual match groups. Subpatterns are placed within parentheses to identify each individual matched group across the data set. In this example, match groups are demonstrated by matching each of the three sections of a domain name into their own group.

To start, the data set is identified and then the regexp.MustCompile() function is used to define the pattern. The pattern uses the \w+ syntax to match one or more word characters on either side of the dot. Then, using the dataset as input, the regexp.Regexp.FindAllStringSubmatch() method is called to return a two-dimensional slice, where the first slice value is the entire set of matches and each consecutive value is the respective matched group. A -1 is used as an input to the regexp.Regexp.FindAllStringSubmatch() method which signifies unlimited matches; otherwise, a positive number could have been set to limit the result.

```
package main

import (
    "fmt"
    "regexp"
)

func main() {
    data := `# host.domain.tld #`
```

```
    pattern := regexp.MustCompile(`(\w+).(\w+).(\w+)`)

    groups := pattern.FindAllStringSubmatch( data, -1)

    fmt.Printf("\n%q\n", groups)
    fmt.Printf("groups[0][0]: %s\n", groups[0][0])
    fmt.Printf("groups[0][1]: %s\n", groups[0][1])
    fmt.Printf("groups[0][2]: %s\n", groups[0][2])
    fmt.Printf("groups[0][3]: %s\n", groups[0][3])
}
```

The output below first demonstrates the entire match, followed by
each individual group.

```
[["host.domain.tld" "host" "domain" "tld"]]
groups[0][0]: host.domain.tld
groups[0][1]: host
groups[0][2]: domain
groups[0][3]: tld
```

8.3: Named Capture Groups

When a regular expression becomes complicated, it is helpful to document and reference the purpose of each capture group by name. Since group names and positions are fixed, they can be referenced using the regexp.Regexp.SubExpNames() method. The group index within the slice matches the corresponding index in the slice that is returned by the regexp.Regexp.FindStringSubmatch() method, which is then used to build a map as demonstrated in the example below.

This example first identifies the data set and then uses the regexp.MustCompile() function to define the pattern. The pattern uses the \w+ syntax to match one or more word characters on either side of the dot. Since named capture groups are used, each pattern is defined with the (?P<name>re) syntax, where name is the capture group name.

Then, using the dataset as input, the regexp.Regexp.FindStringSubmatch() method is called to return a slice, where the first slice value is the leftmost match. Next, a map is created to hold the result and then the slice that is returned from the regexp.Regexp.SubExpNames() method is looped over, which returns each name of the parenthesized subexpressions. As each name is iterated over, the subexpression name is checked to ensure it is not empty. If the name is valid, the map entry is created using the name as the key and the corresponding submatch index value as the value, before finally printing the new map.

```go
package main

import (
    "fmt"
    "regexp"
)

func main() {
    dat := `# host.domain.tld #`

    pat := regexp.MustCompile(
        `(?P<third>(\w+)).(?P<sec>(\w+)).(?P<first>(\w+))`)

    mch := pat.FindStringSubmatch(dat)

    res := make(map[string]string)

    for i, name := range pat.SubexpNames() {
        if i != 0 && name != "" {
            res[name] = mch[i]
        }
    }

    ff := fmt.Printf
    ff("\n%q\n", res)
    ff("res[\"first\"]: %s\n", res["first"])
    ff("res[\"sec\"]: %s\n", res["sec"])
    ff("res[\"third\"]: %s\n", res["third"])
}
```

The output below first demonstrates the entire match, followed by each value that is referenced by the named match key in the result map.

```
map["third":"host" "sec":"domain" "first":"tld"]
result["first"]: tld
result["sec"]: domain
result["third"]: host
```

8.4: Template Expansion

Template expansion captures regular expression pattern matches and expands them into a string template. This example demonstrates template expansion by using the regexp.Regexp.ExpandString() method to take a group of matches from the regular expression and expand them into the template.

To begin the example, the data set is identified as the source and then the regexp.MustCompile() function is used to define the pattern. The pattern uses the \w+ syntax to match one or more word characters on either side of the dot. Next, the string template is defined. It takes the named match as a variable by prefixing it with a dollar sign. Then, each matched line is looped over and returned from the regexp.Regexp.FindAllStringSubmatchIndex() method. Each match is then expanded into the template by using the regexp.Regexp.ExpandString() method to produce the output.

```
package main

import (
    "fmt"
    "regexp"
)

func main() {
    src := `
host1.domain.tld some text
host2.domain.tld more text
`
```

```
re := regexp.MustCompile(
    `(?m)(?P<thir>\w+).(?P<sec>\w+).(?P<fir>\w+)\s(?P<text>.*)$`)

tpl := "$thir.$sec.$fir.\tIN\tTXT\t\"$text\"\n"

dst := []byte{}

findidx := re.FindAllStringSubmatchIndex
for _, matches := range findidx(src, -1) {
    dst = re.ExpandString(dst, tpl, src, matches)
}
fmt.Println(string(dst))
}
```

The output below demonstrates the list of data in template form.

```
host1.domain.tld.
host2.domain.tld.
```

8.5: Multi-line Delimited Split

A multi-line delimited split is useful for extracting lines of text that are separated by a pattern, such as sections in a configuration. It can be used to enable inventory, auditing, or managing configurations. The multi-line m flag causes the ^ and $ regexp syntax to additionally match the beginning and end of each line.

This example splits the defined configuration into a two-dimensional slice, where each of the configuration sections that are delimited by the ! character is represented by its own slice. Each line of configuration is then represented as a string within the respective configuration section slice.

To begin, the configuration is defined and then the pattern is used as a parameter in the regexp.MustCompile() function to return a regexp.Regexp object. Next, the regexp.Regex.Split() method is called on the object using the configuration and -1 to process unlimited matches. This method splits the configuration into a single slice, where each value is what remains between the pattern matches.

After initializing the two-dimensional slice, the values that are returned from splitting the configuration are iterated over. Finally, within the loop, the trailing new-line character is trimmed with the strings.TrimSuffix() function and then each string is split by their new-line character, returning and then appending a new slice with values returned from splitting each line.

```go
package main

import (
    "fmt"
    "regexp"
    "strings"
)

func main() {
    config := `int Vlan1
  desc v1
!
int Vlan2
  desc v2
`

    a := regexp.MustCompile("(?m)(\n^!$\n)")
    m := a.Split(config, -1)

    arr := [][]string{}

    for _, s := range m {
        s := strings.TrimSuffix(s, "\n")
        m := strings.Split(s, "\n")

        arr = append(arr, m)
    }

    fmt.Printf("%q\n", arr)
}
```

The output is shown with double quotes and brackets to demonstrate the result.

```
[["int Vlan1" " desc v1"]["int Vlan2" " desc v2"]]
```

9

External Commands

Executing external commands leverages the exec package to wrap the os.StartProcess function which makes it easier to remap the terminal stdout and stderr pipes. While the exec.Command() function is straightforward to use on external commands, care must be taken to handle terminal redirection.

This chapter works through examples that demonstrate combining stderr and stdout and another that separates the two. Having the choice to natively handle redirection can lend itself to cleanliness and readability.

This chapter will cover the following external command topics:

- Combined Stdout/Stderr
- Separate Stdout/Stderr

9.1: Combined Stdout/Stderr

The exec package supports the ability to combine the terminal standard output and error after a command has executed. This combined output can streamline output processing and save several steps.

A scenario will be setup to demonstrate where two files will be created; one that is writable and the other where write privileges are removed. Using the cat command, we will read each of the files and expect the to see the standard output from the readable file (r.txt) and the standard error from the non-readable file (w.txt).

```
$ touch r.txt w.txt
$ echo hi from r.txt > r.txt
$ chmod a-r w.txt
```

To start, the command and parameters are entered as separate string arguments to the exec.Command() function which returns an exec.Cmd object. Next, the exec.Cmd.CombinedOutput() method is called to execute the command and return the combined standard output and error. Finally, the returned byte slice is printed.

```
package main

import (
    "fmt"
    "os/exec"
)
```

```go
func main() {
    cmd := exec.Command("cat", "r.txt", "w.txt")

    data, _ := cmd.CombinedOutput()

    fmt.Printf("%s", data)
}
```

Take note that the output first displays the standard output text from the readable file (r.txt) and then the error text from the non-readable file (w.txt).

```
hi from r.txt
cat: w.txt: Permission denied
```

9.2: Separate Stdout/Stderr

This example will show how to execute a command and separate the standard terminal output and error. The exec package easily executes external commands and distinguishes between standard output and standard error through its native functions.

Similar to the previous section, a scenario will be setup to demonstrate. Two files will be created; one that is writable and the other where write privileges are removed. Using the cat command, we will read each of the files and expect the to see the standard output from the readable file (r.txt) and the standard error from the non-readable file (w.txt).

```
$ touch r.txt w.txt
$ echo hi from r.txt > r.txt
$ chmod a-r w.txt
```

To start, the command and parameters are entered as separate string arguments to the exec.Command() function which returns an exec.Cmd object. Next, each pipe is assigned that will connect to the terminal standard output and error when the command starts. Then, the command is started with the exec.Cmd.Start() method and the ioutil.ReadAll() function is leveraged to read the io.ReadCloser object that is returned from the pipes before printing the output. Finally, the exec.Cmd.Wait() method is used to close the pipe after seeing the command exit.

```go
package main

import (
    "fmt"
    "io/ioutil"
    "os/exec"
)

func main() {
    cmd := exec.Command("cat", "r.txt", "w.txt")

    stdoutpipe, _ := cmd.StdoutPipe()
    stderrpipe, _ := cmd.StderrPipe()

    _ = cmd.Start()

    stdout, _ := ioutil.ReadAll(stdoutpipe)
    stderr, _ := ioutil.ReadAll(stderrpipe)

    fmt.Printf("stdout: %sstderr: %s", stdout, stderr)

    _ = cmd.Wait()
}
```

The output first displays the standard output text from the readable file (r.txt) and then the error text from the non-readable file (w.txt).

```
stdout: hi from r.txt
stderr: cat: w.txt: Permission denied
```

10

CLI Application Helpers

CLI application helpers are used as building blocks in command-line applications. These are helpful for quickly and easily construct interactive programs.

This chapter will cover three different methods for reading in data. User input from a prompt is demonstrated for sensitive and non-sensitive data, followed by command-line arguments and flags for in-line parameters. Finally, column formatted output is examined to demonstrate an effective pattern to present data.

This chapter will cover the following CLI application helper topics:

- User input
- Command-line arguments
- Command-line flags
- Column ormatting

10.1: User Input

Reading user input from the terminal is often needed to read in both sensitive and non-sensitive data. This example takes in a username and a password to demonstrate the two. To keep it short, the terminal.ReadPassword() function will be used to read the sensitive password text from the terminal without local echo. The bufio.Reader.Readstring() method will be used for non-sensitive input.

This example starts by reading the non-sensitive username input by wrapping os.Stdin with the bufio.NewReader() function to return a buffered bufio.Reader object. Then, the prompt is printed and the bufio.Reader.Readstring() method is called while using a new-line character as the argument. This will return the input as a string prior to the new-line. Next, the sensitive password prompt is printed and the terminal.ReadPassword() function is called using syscall.Stdin as an argument to disable local echo and retrieve the password. Finally, the username and password are printed as validation.

```
package main

import (
    "bufio"
    "fmt"
    "golang.org/x/crypto/ssh/terminal"
    "os"
    "syscall"
)
```

```go
func main() {
    reader := bufio.NewReader(os.Stdin)

    fmt.Print("Enter username: ")
    user, _ := reader.ReadString('\n')

    fmt.Print("Enter password: ")
    pass, _ := terminal.ReadPassword(int(syscall.Stdin))

    fmt.Printf("\n\nUsername: %sPassword: %s\n", user, string(pass))
}
```

The output displays the username and password prompts and then the output of the result below. The password is not displayed when the user types it in to avoid shoulder surfing.

```
Enter username: John Doe
Enter password:

Username: John Doe
Password: $ecret
```

10.2: Command-line Arguments

Command-line arguments are a common method to add parameters to the execution of programs. This example leverages the os.Args slice that holds each command-line argument, where the first value is the executing program name and the rest are the arguments.

In the example program, only two user actions are allowed, add or delete. As a result, only three arguments are accepted, (1) the program itself, (2) the keywords "add" or "del", and (3) the item that is acted on.

First, the total number of command-line arguments is validated by checking if the length is anything other than three, if so, the help dialog is printed and program is exited. Next, since the "add" or "del" keywords are the only two accepted as the second argument, a switch and case statement is used on the second argument, continuing with the corresponding action, else displaying the help dialog and exiting.

```
package main

import (
    "fmt"
    "os"
)
```

```go
func main() {
    if len(os.Args) != 3 {
        fmt.Printf("usage: %s add|del \n", os.Args[0])
        os.Exit(1)
    }

    switch os.Args[1] {
    case "add":
        fmt.Println("adding item")
    case "del":
        fmt.Println("deleting item")
    default:
        fmt.Printf("usage: %s add|del \n", os.Args[0])
        os.Exit(1)
    }
}
```

10. 3: Command-line Flags

Command-line flags are another common method to specify options for command-line programs. This example uses the flag package to demonstrate parsing arguments and will parse int, bool, and string types. By default, the flag package will accept a "-h" or "--help" flag to display the help dialog. If no flag value is entered the default value, defined as the second flag parameter, is assigned.

In the first section of the example, the flags are declared using the appropriate flag function according to the type. Next, the flag name is specified, the default value, and usage string. Then, after all flags are defined, the flag.Parse() function is called to parse the command line user input into the defined flags. Finally, the flag values are accessed as pointers.

```go
package main

import (
    "flag"
    "fmt"
)

func main() {
    port := flag.Int("p", 8000,
        "specify port. default is 8000.")

    enable := flag.Bool("e", false,
        "specify enable. default is false.")
```

```
    name := flag.String("n", "blank",
        "specify name. default is blank.")

    flag.Parse()

    fmt.Println("port = ", *port)
    fmt.Println("enable = ", *enable)
    fmt.Println("name = ", *name)
}
```

The program is ran from the local directory using flags as input. The output displays the flag values.

```
$ ./program -p 80 -e true -n test

port = 80
enable = true
name = test
```

10. 4: Column Formatting

Command-line application output is often viewed in column format to correlate items. The tabwriter package enables easy formatting of columns using tab-terminated cells in contiguous lines.

The example starts out by allocating and initializing a new tabwriter.Writer object. The parameters, from left to right are used for output, min-width, tab-width, padding, padding-character, and custom flags (e.g., right-alignment). Next, the fmt.Fprintf function is used to format the columns and write to the tabwriter.Writer object. Finally, the tabwriter.Writer.Flush() method is used after the last call to ensure that any buffered data is written to the output.

```
package main

import (
    "fmt"
    "os"
    "text/tabwriter"
)

func main() {
    w := tabwriter.NewWriter(
        os.Stdout, 8, 8, 0, '\t', 0)

    fmt.Fprintf(w, "\n %s\t%s\t%s\t",
        "Col1", "Col2", "Col3")

    fmt.Fprintf(w, "\n %s\t%s\t%s\t",
        "----", "----", "----")
```

```
    for i := 0; i < 5; i++ {
        fmt.Fprintf(
            w, "\n %d\t%d\t%d\t", i, i+1, i+2)
    }
    w.Flush()
}
```

The output displays the left justified three-column format.

```
Col1    Col2    Col3
----    ----    ----
0       1       2
1       2       3
2       3       4
3       4       5
4       5       6
```

www.ingramcontent.com/pod-product-compliance
Lightning Source LLC
Chambersburg PA
CBHW070843070326
40690CB00009B/1679